Look

A Reading Anthology for Young Learners

KAJ SCHWERMER

NATIONAL GEOGRAPHIC
LEARNING

Australia • Brazil • Mexico • Singapore • United Kingdom • United States

Contents

STORY 1

The Stars of Salta

Like any child growing up in the town of Salta in Argentina, Mateo, Matías, and their younger sister, María, loved folk music. Every evening, they could hear the sound of drums, guitars, and singing from the open windows of the town's music halls.

The music was so wonderful that even the stars above Salta seemed to dance with joy every evening. All three children dreamed of playing in one of the music halls one day.

Mateo and Matías were twin brothers. It was their birthday in June. This year, they had a big party with everyone to celebrate.

As the party ended, they opened their presents from their family and friends. Their uncle gave them a video game. Mateo's best friend gave him a book.

The best present of all was from their grandma: a beautiful new guitar.

Mateo and Matías started to play their new guitar. First Mateo played a tune. Then Matías played one. Everyone cheered.

"Wow! That's great. The twins are playing the guitar!" they shouted.

Their mom started singing, and soon everyone started clapping, laughing, and dancing.

At last, the party finished, and everyone went home. Mateo and Matías looked at each other. "That was fun!" they said.

"Have you seen María?" Mateo asked.

"No, I haven't," Matías replied. "I saw her half an hour ago, but I haven't seen her since then. Let's go and look for her."

Mateo and Matías went up the stairs. María was all alone at the top of the stairs. She looked sad.

"Are you OK? What's wrong?" Mateo and Matías asked María.

María replied, "Oh, it's nothing. I wanted to join you, but I can't play the guitar. I've never played it before."

"I have an idea," said Mateo.

"Oh! What is it?" asked María.

"Let's all go out together tomorrow," replied Mateo. "I'll tell you then."

The next day, they went up San Bernardo Hill in a cable car. They pressed their faces against the glass as they went up.

The view of the town was amazing. The streets and buildings of Salta looked smaller and smaller as the cable car climbed higher and higher. When they looked across the valley, they could see the hills on the other side of the town. The hills seemed to glow as the golden sun went down.

They arrived at the top of the hill and looked down on the town. As the sun went down, the lights of Salta started to come on, one by one. Thousands of orange streetlights stretched out across the valley like a giant, glowing spider's web. The stars above also started to appear, one by one, until they filled the sky. It was magical.

The children enjoyed the view for a while. Then María gave her brothers an envelope.

"Happy Birthday," she said. "I made this for you."

Inside the envelope was a birthday card shaped like a guitar. "We love it!" they replied. "And we have something for you, too!"

Mateo gave a small box to María. Inside was a harmonica with her name on it. María was delighted. "Thank you!"

When they arrived home, Matías showed María how to play the harmonica. Then the three children practiced together. The two brothers played the guitar one after the other, and María played her new harmonica. They practiced every morning before school and every evening after dinner.

Six months later, it was their grandma's birthday. She had a party in the biggest music hall in Salta.

"We have a special surprise for you, Grandma!" said the children. María, Matías, and Mateo played their grandma's favorite folk song. "Bravo, bravo! I love it!" shouted Grandma. They played song after song, and everyone danced all evening. Everyone was happy, especially María and her grandma.

Mateo looked out of the window at the night sky. The stars seemed to dance. He was happy, too.

STORY 2

Penguins on the Beach

The first day of summer vacation is always a special day for Amahle and Bandile. They usually like relaxing at home all day, but today they didn't want to spend the day at home.

The Cape Town sun was shining on the water in False Bay. The children got up early. They wanted to go outside and enjoy the nice South African weather.

After breakfast, Mom asked, "Where do you want to go today?" Bandile and Amahle smiled at each other and said, "The beach!"

Mom looked at Dad. "When you go to Boulders Beach today, can the children go with you?" she asked.

"Of course!" Dad replied. "Let's go!"

Mom turned to the children, but they were already running out the door with their buckets and shovels.

As soon as they arrived at the beach, Bandile and Amahle ran onto the sand and started to dig.

"Sandcastle number one, here we come!" shouted Bandile.

Just as they were starting to dig, they heard a loud noise coming from behind some rocks. It sounded like a donkey.

"What was that?" laughed Bandile.

"Is there a donkey on the beach?" Amahle asked. "Let's take a look."

Amahle, Bandile, and Dad climbed onto the rocks and looked over.

They didn't see any donkeys, but they were amazed at what they saw instead.

Penguins!

"I've never seen penguins on a beach before!" shouted Bandile.

"Shhh! Be quiet, or you'll scare them," Dad whispered. "Those are African Penguins. Their habitat is in Namibia and South Africa. This beach is their home."

"Is their habitat really a beach in a city?" whispered Amahle.

"Yes. They're one of the only types of penguins that like living near towns."

"The first penguins came here in 1983. At first, there were only two, but now there are about 2,000 penguins," replied Dad.

The children watched the penguins for a while from the rocks. The penguins didn't notice a big seagull. It was walking past them towards their nests near the rocks.

Dad saw the seagull and chased it away.

"Seagulls like eating penguin eggs," he said to Bandile and Amahle. "Come with me."

They walked along the beach until they came to a small shack. The sign on the door said "BirdLife South Africa."

"This is where I work," said Dad.

"I knew you worked near a beach, but I've never actually seen where you work," said Bandile. "It's great!"

"Yes," replied Dad. "There are only a few of those African Penguins left in the world. My job is to take care of them."

"The penguin colony was once a lot bigger, but it isn't very big anymore. In fact, the penguins are almost extinct," Dad explained.

"Why is that?" Amahle asked.

"Well, it's complicated," Dad replied. "One reason is that seagulls, wild cats, and other animals eat the penguin eggs. Do you want to help me protect the eggs?"

"Yes, please!" they both replied.

Dad pulled out a penguin nest box from the closet in the shack.

"Come on! Help me take this to the beach," he said.

They put the nest box on a cart and pulled it down to the beach. Then they put it near the penguins.

"The penguins will make their nests in the nest boxes," Dad said. "The seagulls won't be able to eat the penguin eggs as easily."

Later, in the car on the way home, Bandile and Amahle asked Dad a lot of questions about African penguins, and Dad answered all of them.

They learned another reason why the penguins are endangered. The fishermen in the area catch too many fish, so there aren't enough fish left for the penguins to eat.

Every weekend after that, Bandile and Amahle helped their father protect the penguins. They put nest boxes on the beach, they made signs telling fishermen not to fish in the area, and they built a fence to keep wild cats out.

At the end of the summer, they made a video to teach other children about the endangered African Penguins.

It was the best summer ever!

STORY 3

Cao Chong Weighs an Elephant

These days, it's easy to see animals from around the world, but hundreds of years ago, seeing a new animal for the very first time was an amazing event. That's how it was in China when the wise ruler, Sun Quan, received an elephant as a gift from a faraway land.

Sun Quan wondered how much this mysterious new animal weighed. He asked his wisest, most intelligent women and men for advice.

One man stepped forward and said, "We can use some scales."

Sun Quan closed his eyes and thought for a few seconds. Then he replied, "That's a wonderful idea, but there aren't any scales in China as big as this elephant."

Another wise person suggested, "We can build some scales that are big enough to weigh this creature, Your Majesty."

Sun Quan, who was wise as well as practical, replied, "That's a good idea, but how can we be sure that the elephant won't just walk off the scales?"

They discussed the problem for a long time, but no one could think of an answer that made the ruler happy.

Finally, Sun Quan announced, "I've invited the wisest, most intelligent women and men in the land here today. It's clear to me that none of us knows the answer. If no one here can solve this problem, then I officially declare that this problem is too difficult for us to solve. You can all go now."

Just as everyone was leaving, a voice from the back of the crowd cried out, "I know how to weigh the elephant!"

Sun Quan looked up and asked, "Who are you? Please step forward!"

The crowd parted to let the person through. To everyone's surprise, the ruler's six-year-old son stepped forward and repeated, "Daddy, I know how to weigh the elephant!"

Sun Quan laughed when he saw that it was his own son, Cao Chong. He said, "Tell us your idea, son. What is it?"

Cao Chong walked up to his father and whispered the idea in his ear.

The ruler listened carefully. Then he smiled and said to the crowd, "Let's go! We will watch the weighing of the elephant by the river."

Everyone followed Cao Chong and his father down to the river where there was a large boat. Cao Chong asked the guards to guide the elephant onto the boat. The elephant walked slowly onto the boat, and as it did, the boat sank lower and lower into the water.

After a while, the boat stopped sinking and leveled off. Cao Chong painted a line on the boat just above the water level.

Then Cao Chong asked the guards to take the elephant off the boat. As they did, the boat gradually came up out of the water again. The crowd watched and scratched their heads. They didn't know what was happening.

The young boy whispered into his father's ear again. Sun Quan looked up and said, "Guards, please bring some rocks from the river bank and carry them onto the boat."

One by one, the guards carried the rocks onto the boat.

Again, at first, no one really understood what was happening. As the boat started to sink back into the water, a few people gasped and shouted, "Ah! Now I understand!"

By the time the water level reached the painted line again, everyone understood and was shouting, "What a great idea!"

The people now realized what the boy knew all along: when the guards removed the rocks from the boat and weighed them, they weighed the same as the elephant!

Cao Chong became a hero, not only in his town, but across the whole country. Even today, people around the world talk about him and how smart he was.

STORY 4

The Phoenix and the Carpet

It all began on a cold November morning with a secondhand carpet, rolled up neatly on the bedroom floor, in a house in London.

Cyril, Anthea, Robert, Jane, and their baby brother watched as their mother and father unrolled the dusty old carpet.

They were just as surprised as their parents to see something roll out of the carpet onto the floor.

Robert picked it up. "Look everyone! It's an egg!" he shouted.

Jane tapped the egg. "It's glowing!" she said.

She put the egg safely on the shelf above the fireplace.

A few days later, when the children were playing, Robert accidentally bumped the egg, and it fell into the fire.

The egg opened, and a beautiful flame-colored bird appeared. It was an amazing sight. The children were so shocked they couldn't say anything—all except Robert.

"I know who you are," he said. "You're the Phoenix!"

And, to their surprise, the Phoenix talked back!

They talked to the Phoenix all night.

"The carpet is magic," the Phoenix said. "It will give you three wishes every day. It will take you wherever you want to go."

The children had some exciting adventures on the carpet. Then one day, they decided to go somewhere really amazing.

They decided to go to India! They wanted to get some interesting things for their mother to give to the school sale.

"Please take us where we will find a lot of beautiful Indian things," they asked the carpet.

The carpet moved, and then the world started spinning. Suddenly, the children arrived in a town in India.

As they were walking around the narrow streets, a man appeared and invited them to meet the queen in her palace.

When they arrived at the palace, the queen asked to buy the children's carpet. To her surprise, the children said, "We're sorry. We don't want to sell our carpet."

The queen asked why. So Cyril told the story of the carpet and the Phoenix, and all their adventures.

The queen was so impressed by Cyril's storytelling that she gave them some jewels.

"Oh, how pretty!" cried Jane and Anthea. "Thank you very much. Your gift is wonderful. Mother will be very happy."

The queen gave them many other beautiful things, and they flew back home on the carpet. Their mother was very happy to see them again. She loved all their gifts from India.

For their next adventure, the children decided that they wanted to help someone.

So after breakfast, the four children and the Phoenix got back on the carpet. Cyril made a wish. "Please, will you take us somewhere where we can do something good and kind?"

The carpet moved, and they were off again! Then suddenly, everyone landed in a heap on the floor. It was very dark. They were in a room in a castle. The room was full of treasure!

They opened a trap door and went outside. They were in France!

Anthea asked, "Why did the carpet bring us here? What kind thing are we going to do?"

Cyril answered, "I think we should find the owners of the treasure and tell them about it."

So they walked down the road. The first house they saw was a small white house with green shutters.

Cyril knocked on the door. A woman opened it and invited them in.

They talked to the woman and her son and asked her who owned the castle.

"The castle belongs to our family," she said. "But we have to sell it because we don't have any money. We're going to sell it tomorrow."

The children told the woman about the treasure in the castle.

"Oh, thank you!" cried the woman. "You're so kind. Now we don't have to sell the castle!"

The children had many other wonderful adventures with the Phoenix and the carpet, but in the end, they had to say goodbye to the Phoenix.

They were very sad, but that night a big wooden box arrived at their house. Inside the box was beautiful Chinese paper, and under the paper were all kinds of gifts.

There was everything the children loved—toys, games, books, and chocolate ... and much more.

At the bottom of the box was a tiny golden feather. No one saw it except Robert. He picked it up and put it in his jacket pocket, where the Phoenix used to go when they went on their adventures together.

When Robert went to bed that night, the feather was gone.

It was the last he ever saw of the Phoenix.

STORY
5

The Legend of Urashima Taro

A long time ago, in a small fishing village in Japan, lived a young fisherman called Urashima Taro. The life of a fisherman in those days was hard. Every morning, Urashima Taro had to get up very early to clean his boat and prepare his nets.

One morning, as he was cleaning his boat, Urashima Taro saw a turtle trapped in his net. He gently helped the turtle out of the net, and off it went, back to its home in the ocean.

Later that day, Urashima Taro was fishing far out in the ocean when he noticed something swimming towards him. He looked down into the water and saw the turtle from earlier that morning!

The turtle looked up at Urashima Taro and said, "Thank you for saving me. Let me take you to my home under the water. Please ride on my back."

Urashima Taro climbed onto the turtle's back. They swam down until they arrived at a large gate at the bottom of the ocean.

The turtle turned to Urashima Taro and said, "Here we are. If you go through that gate, you will come to the palace of the sea king. You must walk from here."

Urashima Taro thanked the turtle and walked up to the gate.

Before he had time to knock, the gate slowly opened. Urashima Taro was amazed at what he saw.

In front of him was a magnificent coral palace. It had pearls and shells on its walls, and hundreds of colorful fish were swimming in and out of its windows.

A beautiful princess came out to greet him. "Welcome to the palace of the sea king, Urashima Taro," she said.

"How do you know my name?" asked Urashima Taro. "Have we met before?"

"Yes, we have," she said. "This morning you helped a turtle. That turtle was me! You saved my life. If you like, you can live here in this magical kingdom, where you will be happy and young forever."

So Urashima Taro, the poor, young fisherman, decided to stay in this magical place.

It was like a dream. Every day there were new wonders for Urashima Taro. He was so happy that he forgot everything, even his home and his family in the poor fishing village.

Three days later, as Urashima Taro was sitting all alone, he started to worry about his family and friends back in his little village.

He said to the princess, "I'm sorry. I have to go home now. My family and friends are waiting for me."

“I’m sad that you’re leaving,” said the princess. “Please take this small gift back with you.” She gave him a small box.

“Thank you. What is it?” Urashima Taro asked.

“This box contains something very precious,” answered the princess. “If you open it, something terrible will happen to you. Now promise me that you will never open this box!”

“I promise,” said Urashima Taro.

Urashima Taro took the box and rode on the turtle's back up to his village again.

When Urashima Taro got back to his village, he didn't recognize anyone. Everything looked different. His house wasn't there. His friends and family weren't there.

"That's strange," he said to himself. "I was only in the underwater kingdom for three days. Why is everything different?"

Urashima Taro didn't know what to do. He was very sad and lonely. He decided to open the box. He didn't remember his promise.

He slowly opened the lid. White smoke came out, and Urashima Taro turned into an old man with white hair.

Finally, Urashima Taro realized the truth. In fact, he was in the underwater kingdom for 300 years!

Then Urashima Taro noticed a small drawer in the box. Inside there was a white feather. He picked it up, and as he did, he turned into a beautiful white crane.

A turtle looked up quietly from the ocean far below. She saw the crane flying high in the sky.

Next time you see a white crane flying above the ocean, remember the legend of Urashima Taro, the young Japanese fisherman.

STORY 6

Stephanie Kwolek: Scientist, Inventor, Pioneer

Car tire

Cable

Canoe

What do skis, canoes, fiber optic cables, frying pans, car tires, snare drums, hockey sticks, body armor, firefighter gloves, and suspension bridge cables all have in common?

They're all made from an amazing kind of fiber that is five times stronger than steel but as light as plastic called Kevlar.

This special type of plastic was invented by a young woman named Stephanie Kwolek.

So who was Stephanie Kwolek, and how did she become a pioneer and role model for so many other female scientists and inventors?

Stephanie Kwolek was born in 1923 in Pennsylvania in the U.S. Her love of nature and science began when she was a child. Her parents were both from Poland, and her father enjoyed studying nature. She loved exploring the woods and fields around her home in Pennsylvania with him.

"I loved learning new things and making new discoveries," said Stephanie.

Stephanie collected leaves, wildflowers, seeds, and grasses and kept them in her scrapbook. She used to spend hours carefully describing and classifying everything she collected.

Stephanie also loved sewing with her mother, who was a seamstress. She really loved fabrics and textiles, and Stephanie used to spend many hours designing and making clothes for her dolls. For a while, she wanted to become a fashion designer, but she ended up studying chemistry instead. She wanted to become a doctor.

Carnegie Mellon University

When Stephanie graduated from college in 1946, she didn't have enough money to pay for medical school, so she decided to get a job. She wanted a job where she could do research.

Stephanie was interviewed for a job at the chemical company DuPont and was offered a job as a researcher in textile chemistry. She enjoyed her work there and continued to work at DuPont for many years. She was one of the few female scientists working there after the end of World War II.

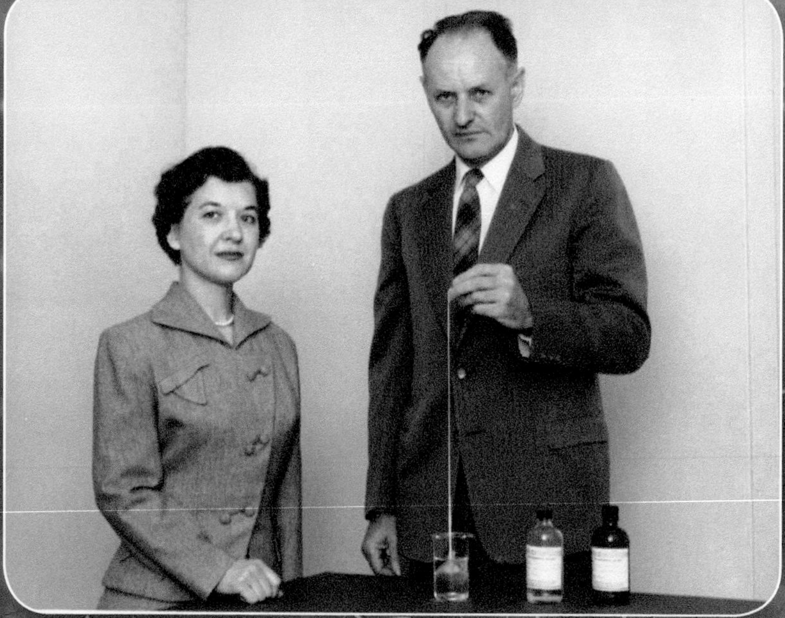

In 1964, scientists at DuPont started to research a new lightweight fiber to use in tires. The project didn't seem very interesting, so very few people wanted to work on it. However, Stephanie decided to join the project.

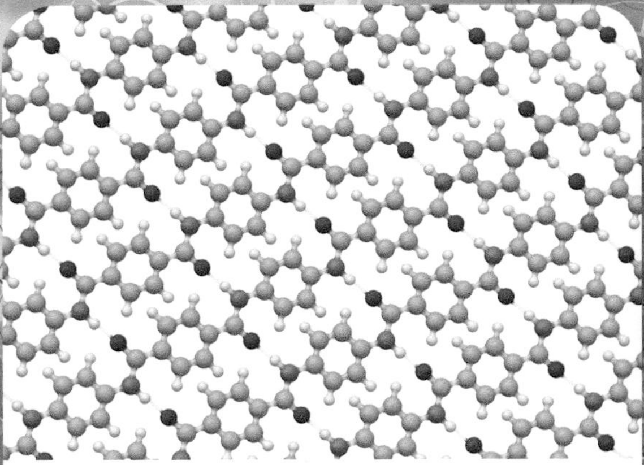

Molecular structure of Kevlar

The researchers on Stephanie's team were finding it difficult to develop a stronger type of fiber. Then one day, in 1965, while Stephanie was working in her lab, an unexpected discovery was made—a new type of plastic! This plastic was later called Kevlar.

Modern spinneret machine making Kevlar fiber

At the time, most plastic mixtures that were used to make new fibers were thick and clear like syrup. The mixture that was created by Stephanie, however, was cloudy and fluid like water.

"There's something different about this. This may be very useful," Stephanie thought. They put the new liquid plastic in a machine called a spinneret to make the fiber, and the result was amazing.

Fabric made of Kevlar

Other fibers often broke, but Stephanie's fibers were much stiffer and stronger. Stephanie was interviewed years later, and she said, "I was very excited. We were all looking for something new. Something different. And this was it!"

Stephanie was awarded a medal by her company for her amazing discovery. She was the first and only woman to receive this award.

Kevlar is used in firefighter clothing, helmets, and hoses.

Kevlar is used in sails.

Although it was originally developed for tires, nowadays Kevlar is found in hundreds of products that we all use every day. Because it is so strong and light, Kevlar is used in a lot of safety equipment, from helmets to safety gloves. Since it was invented, Kevlar has saved the lives of many people.

Kevlar is used to make cables stronger.

Kevlar is used in astronaut suits.

Kevlar is used in underwater fiber optic cables.

The Kevlar fiber is also used in a lot of sports equipment. It is used in hockey sticks and tennis rackets instead of wood, as it is lighter and stronger than wood. It is also used in products for space exploration.

A high-strength material that is very similar to Kevlar is used in the underwater fiber optic cables that connect us all to the Internet. It was discovered that sharks were chewing the cables, so this Kevlar-like layer was added to protect them.

Since her creation of Kevlar, Stephanie Kwolek has received many more awards for her achievements. Her name is in the National Inventors Hall of Fame, only the fourth woman ever. She has won the National Medal of Technology and many other prizes. The true reward of her work, however, are the many lives she has saved by her invention.

After she retired in 1986, she spent her time teaching high school students, especially girls, who were interested in chemistry. She traveled around the country giving talks at schools, hoping to inspire the next generation of women scientists and inventors. Maybe someday that will be you!

STORY 1 The Stars of Salta

1 Order the sentences from 1 to 6.

A. The twins gave María a harmonica. ☐

B. María was all alone at the top of the stairs. ☐

C. The children played their grandma's favorite folk song at her party. ☐

D. The children went up San Bernardo Hill in a cable car. ☐

E. Mateo and Matías had a big birthday party. 1

F. The children practiced together. ☐

2 Read and circle.

1. Like any child growing up in Salta, Mateo, Matías, and María:
   A. played the guitar.
   B. had a party every evening.
   C. loved folk music.
2. Mateo and Matías's grandma gave them:
   A. a harmonica. B. a guitar. C. a book.
3. María was sad at the party because:
   A. she wanted to play the guitar with her brothers.
   B. she wanted to play her harmonica.
   C. the party was too loud.
4. María gave her brothers a birthday card shaped like:
   A. a star. B. a book. C. a guitar.
5. In the end, the children played music together:
   A. at their grandma's birthday party.
   B. in the cable car.
   C. at the top of San Bernardo Hill.

3 Read and complete the sentences.

~~dreamed~~ arrived practiced gave played started

1. They dreamed ______ of playing in one of the music halls one day.
2. Mateo's best friend ______ him a book.
3. The twins ______ their new guitar at their birthday party.
4. They ______ at the top of the hill and looked down on the town.
5. The stars ______ to appear, one by one.
6. They ______ every morning before school and every evening after dinner.

4 Answer the questions.

1. Which country is Salta in?

______

2. What did the stars above Salta seem to do every evening?

______

3. When was Matías and Mateo's birthday?

______

4. Where did Matías and Mateo find María after the party?

______

5. Where did the children go the day after the party?

______

6. What did Matías and Mateo give María?

______

STORY 2

Penguins on the Beach

1 Read and write T (true) or F (false).

1. Amahle and Bandile wanted to spend the first day of summer vacation at home. F
2. As soon as the children arrived at the beach, they started to build a sandcastle. ______
3. There were some donkeys on the beach. ______
4. Many types of penguins like living near towns. ______
5. The penguin colony was once big, but it isn't anymore. ______
6. The children built a fence to keep the wild animals out. ______
7. The seagulls will make their nests in the nest boxes. ______
8. The fishermen in the area don't catch enough fish. ______

2 Find the words in bold in the story. Circle the meaning.

1. A **beach** is a place near the *ocean* / *mountains.*
2. A **habitat** is a place or area where animals *visit* / *live.*
3. A **colony** is *a group of penguins* / *what penguins eat.*
4. When an animal becomes **extinct**, it *disappears* / *becomes ill.*
5. When you **protect** something, you *take care of it* / *chase it away.*
6. If an animal is **endangered**, it is *safe* / *at risk.*

3 Answer the questions.

1. What did the children see on the beach?

   ____

2. What do the African Penguins sound like?

   ____

3. Where's the African Penguins' habitat?

   ____

4. What does Amahle and Bandile's dad do for a job?

   ____

5. Why are the African Penguins almost extinct? Give two reasons.

   ____

6. How did the children help protect the penguins?

   ____

4 Match the problems with the children's solutions.

1. Seagulls eat the penguin eggs.
2. The fishermen catch too many fish.
3. Wild cats eat the penguin eggs.
4. Other children don't know about the African Penguins.

A. Make a video to teach other children about the penguins.
B. Put nest boxes on the beach.
C. Build a fence to keep wild cats and other animals out.
D. Make signs telling fishermen not to fish in the area.

STORY 3

Cao Chong Weighs an Elephant

1 Order the sentences from 1 to 6.

A. The elephant walked slowly onto the boat. ☐

B. The guards weighed the rocks from the boat. ☐

C. Sun Quan received an elephant as a gift from a faraway land. 1

D. The guards carried the rocks onto the boat. ☐

E. Cao Chong painted a line on the boat just above the water level. ☐

F. Cao Chong had an idea about how to weigh the elephant. ☐

2 Read and write T (true) or F (false).

1. There were many elephants in Sun Quan's town. F
2. Sun Quan had some scales that were as big as the elephant. ______
3. The most intelligent people in the land couldn't solve the problem. ______
4. Sun Quan didn't listen to his son's idea. ______
5. When the elephant walked onto the boat, it sank lower into the water. ______
6. The guards carried a lot of cushions onto the boat. ______
7. At first, no one understood what was happening. ______
8. People still talk about Cao Chong today. ______

3 Read and complete the sentences.

received whispered painted watched carried ~~weighed~~

1. The guards removed the rocks from the boat and weighed them.
2. Sun Quan ______________ an elephant as a gift from a faraway land.
3. Cao Chong ______________ a line on the boat just above the water level.
4. One by one, the guards ______________ the rocks onto the boat.
5. Cao Chong ______________ the idea in his father's ear.
6. The crowd ______________ and scratched their heads.

4 Answer the questions.

1. What did Sun Quan want to find out about the elephant?

   ____

2. Who did Sun Quan ask for advice?

   ____

3. Where did they go to weigh the elephant?

   ____

4. Where did Cao Chong paint a line?

   ____

5. What did the guards carry onto the boat?

   ____

6. How much did all of the rocks weigh?

   ____

STORY 4

The Phoenix and the Carpet

1 Order the sentences from 1 to 6.

A. The queen in India asked to buy the children's carpet. ☐

B. Next, the children went on the carpet to France. ☐

C. The egg opened, and a beautiful flame-colored bird appeared. 1

D. A big wooden box full of gifts arrived at their house. ☐

E. The children rode on the carpet to a town in India. ☐

F. The children told the woman about the treasure in the castle. ☐

2 Answer the questions.

1. What rolled out of the dusty, old carpet?

____

2. What appeared after the egg fell into the fire?

____

3. Who did they meet in India?

____

4. What did they find in the dark room in the castle in France?

____

5. Who did the children help when they were in France?

____

6. What was at the bottom of the box that arrived at their house?

____

3 Read and circle.

1. The children put the egg:
   A. in a wooden box. B. above the fireplace.
   C. in a cabinet.
2. The Phoenix said the carpet could:
   A. give you three wishes. B. give you one wish every day.
   C. give you three wishes every day.
3. The children wanted to go to India to:
   A. do something good. B. get some things for their mother.
   C. sell the carpet.
4. In France, the children decided to:
   A. keep the treasure. B. give the treasure to their mother.
   C. find the owners of the treasure.
5. The big wooden box that arrived at their house was full of:
   A. all kinds of gifts. B. treasure. C. eggs.

4 Read and write T (true) or F (false).

1. The carpet their mother and father unrolled was brand new. F
2. The children were shocked to see the Phoenix. ______
3. The children talked to the Phoenix all night. ______
4. The children gave the carpet to the queen in India. ______
5. The woman in France wanted to sell the castle. ______
6. Robert put the tiny golden feather in his jacket pocket. ______

STORY 5

The Legend of Urashima Taro

1 Order the sentences from 1 to 8.

A. One morning, Urashima Taro saw a turtle trapped in his net. [1]

B. Urashima Taro turned into a beautiful white crane. [ ]

C. After three days, Urashima Taro started to worry and decided to go home. [ ]

D. Urashima Taro climbed onto the turtle's back, and they swam down into the ocean. [ ]

E. The princess invited Urashima Taro to stay in the magical kingdom. [ ]

F. A beautiful princess came out of the coral palace to greet him. [ ]

G. Urashima Taro opened the box the princess gave him. [ ]

H. The gate at the bottom of the ocean opened. [ ]

2 Read and write T (true) or F (false).

1. Urashima Taro saved the princess's life. __T__
2. At first, Urashima Taro was happy in the magical kingdom. ______
3. Urashima Taro worried about his family and friends. ______
4. The princess gave him a special shell. ______
5. Everyone in his village was very happy to see him. ______
6. When Urashima Taro picked up the white feather, he turned into a turtle. ______

3 Read and complete.

swimming fishing ~~cleaning~~ sitting saw noticed started

1. As he was cleaning his boat, Urashima Taro ____________ a turtle trapped in his net.
2. Urashima Taro was ____________ far out in the ocean when he ____________ something swimming towards him.
3. Hundreds of colorful fish were ____________ in and out of its windows.
4. As Urashima Taro was ____________ all alone, he ____________ to worry about his family and friends.

4 Answer the questions.

1. What did Urashima Taro see in the water when he was fishing?

   ____

2. What did the princess give Urashima Taro before he went home?

   ____

3. What did Urashima Taro promise never to do?

   ____

4. How long did Urashima Taro think he stayed in the underwater kingdom?

   ____

5. How long did Urashima Taro actually stay in the underwater kingdom?

   ____

STORY 6

Stephanie Kwolek: Scientist, Inventor, Pioneer

1 Answer the questions.

1. Who was Kevlar invented by? Stephanie Kwolek
2. What is Kevlar five times stronger than?
____
3. What did Stephanie want to become when she was a child?
____
4. What did Stephanie do after she graduated from college?
____
5. Why is Kevlar used in a lot of sports equipment?
____
6. What did Stephanie do after she retired?
____

2 Read and complete.

awarded ~~interviewed~~ discovered used found developed

1. Kwolek was interviewed for a job at the chemical company DuPont.
2. Kwolek was ______________ a medal by her company for her amazing discovery.
3. Kevlar was originally ______________ for tires.
4. Kevlar is ______________ in hundreds of products.
5. Kevlar is ______________ in a lot of safety equipment.
6. It was ______________ that sharks were chewing the cables.

3 Read and circle *True* or *False*.

1. When Stephanie Kwolek was a child, she loved nature.
   True *False*
2. Stephanie studied fashion design in college.
   True *False*
3. There were a lot of female scientists at Dupont at the end of World War II.
   True *False*
4. The mixture that was created by Kwolek was fluid and cloudy.
   True *False*
5. The fiber that Kwolek created broke when it was tested.
   True *False*
6. Stephanie has received many awards.
   True *False*

4 Match the dates with the events.

1. 1923	**A.** Stephanie Kwolek retired.
2. 1946	**B.** An unexpected discovery was made.
3. 1964	**C.** Stephanie Kwolek was born.
4. 1965	**D.** Scientists at Dupont started to research a lightweight fiber for tires.
5. 1986	**E.** Stephanie Kwolek graduated from college.

NATIONAL GEOGRAPHIC
LEARNING

National Geographic Learning,
a Cengage Company

Look 5: A Reading Anthology for Young Learners
Kaj Schwermer

Publisher: Sherrise Roehr

Executive Editor: Eugenia Corbo

Publishing Consultant: Karen Spiller

Associate Development Editor: Jen Williams-Rapa

Director of Global Marketing: Ian Martin

Heads of Regional Marketing:

Charlotte Ellis (Europe, Middle East and Africa)

Kiel Hamm (Asia)

Irina Pereyra (Latin America)

Product Marketing Manager: David Spain

Senior Director of Production: Michael Burggren

Senior Content Project Manager: Nick Ventullo

Media Researchers: Leila Hishmeh, Jeff Millies

Art Director: Brenda Carmichael

Manufacturing Planner: Mary Beth Hennebury

Composition: SPi Global

ISBN: 978-0-357-02755-4

National Geographic Learning
5191 Natorp Boulevard
Mason, OH 45040
USA

Locate your local office at **international.cengage.com/region**

Visit National Geographic Learning online at **ELTNGL.com**
Visit our corporate website at **www.cengage.com**

Credits

Cover: Justin Mott

Photos: 3 Hemis/Alamy Stock Photo; **15** © PocholoCalapre/iStock/Getty Images Plus/Getty Images; **27** © Georgi Dimitrov; **39** © vwalakte/iStock/Getty Images Plus/Getty Images; **55** © Doug Perrine/Minden Pictures; **69** Courtesy of the Hagley Museum and Library; **69** (background) © SUWIT NGAOKAEW/Shutterstock.com; **70** (t) © All kind of people/Shutterstock.com; **70** (bl) GREG RYAN/Alamy Stock Photo; **70** (br) PJF Military Collection/Alamy Stock Photo; **70–71** © TLaoPhotography/Shutterstock.com; **71** Courtesy of the Hagley Museum and Library; **72** Courtesy of the Hagley Museum and Library; **72** (background) © CoffeeChocolates/Shutterstock.com; **72–73** © Lukiyanova Natalia frenta/Shutterstock.com; **73** © mickyso/Shutterstock.com; **73** (background) © Lisovskaya Natalia/Shutterstock.com; **74** (t, b) © Carnegie Mellon University; **74–75** © matthew25/Shutterstock.com; **75** © Triff/Shutterstock.com; **76** Courtesy of the Hagley Museum and Library; **76–77** © Sergey Nivens/Shutterstock.com; **77** (t) © theasis/E+/Getty Images; **77** (b) © Javier Larrea/age fotostock/Getty Images; **78** © Monty Rakusen/Cultura/Getty Images; **78–79** © Nik Merkulov/Shutterstock.com; **79** (t) © Archives Center, National Museum of American History, Smithsonian Institution; **79** (b) © TLaoPhotography/Shutterstock.com; **80** (t) © BATMANV/Shutterstock.com; **80** (b) Thornton Cohen/Alamy Stock Photo; **80–81** © meunierd/Shutterstock.com; **81** (t) © NASA/Roger Ressmeyer/Corbis/VCG/Getty Images; **81** (b) © US Navy; **82** Courtesy of the Hagley Museum and Library; **82–83** © TLaoPhotography/Shutterstock.com; **83** © Michael Branscom, courtesy of the Lemelson-MIT Program.

Illustrations: 4–14 Tideway Thaipinnarong/Lemonade Agency; **16–26** Alfredo Belli/Advocate Art; **28–38** Nicholas Castell/Advocate Art; **39–54** Jomike Tejido/MB Artists; **56–68** Mona Meslier Menuau/Advocate Art.

Print Number: 7 Print Year: 2024
Printed in Mexico